The Countries

Kenya

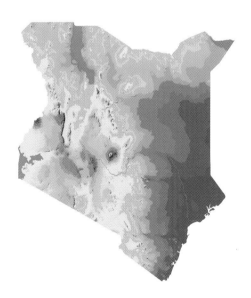

Bob Italia

ABDO Publishing Company

visit us at
www.abdopub.com

Published by ABDO Publishing Company, 4940 Viking Drive, Suite 622, Edina, Minnesota 55435. Copyright © 2000 Abdo Consulting Group, Inc., Pentagon Tower, P.O. Box 36036, Minneapolis, Minnesota 55435 USA. International copyrights reserved in all countries. No part of this book may be reproduced in any form without written permission from the publisher.

Printed in the United States.

Editors: Tamara L. Britton, Kate A. Furlong
Art Direction & Maps: Pat Laurel
Cover & Interior Design: MacLean & Tuminelly (Mpls.)
Interior Photos: Corbis

Library of Congress Cataloging-in-Publication Data

Italia, Bob, 1955-
    Kenya / Bob Italia.
        p. cm. -- (The countries)
Includes index.
ISBN 1-57765-389-0
  1. Kenya--Juvenile literature. [1. Kenya.] I. Title. II. Series.

DT433.522 .I83 2000
967.62--dc21

                                                    00-038108

Contents

Jambo!

Hello from Kenya, the birthplace of the human race. Kenya has the greatest number of large animals left anywhere on Earth. And, there are about 40 national parks and game reserves. They allow visitors to view Kenya's animals in their natural **habitat**.

Kenya's land has much variety. There are deserts, rainforests, grasslands, and snow-capped mountains. Kenya is an unspoiled land. Most of its wealth comes from farming. Tourism is an important part of the **economy**.

Kenya has modern cities. Nairobi is the capital and **cultural** center. It is one of the largest and fastest growing cities in Africa.

Many different kinds of people live in Kenya. There are more than 50 **ethnic** groups speaking close to 80 **dialects**.

Kenya has a long history. For centuries, Arabs and Europeans used its coastal waters for seaports. Great Britain made Kenya a colony in the late 1800s. Only recently has Kenya become an independent nation. Today, Kenya is a meeting place of many cultures trying to live in harmony with its natural wonders.

Jambo *from Kenya!*

Fast Facts

OFFICIAL NAME: Republic of Kenya

CAPITAL: Nairobi

LAND
- Mountain Ranges: Aberdare Range, Mau Escarpment
- Deserts: Chalbi
- Highest Peak: Mount Kenya (17,058 feet/ 5,199 m)
- Major Rivers: Tana, Galana, Turkwel
- Largest Lakes: Lake Turkana, Lake Victoria

PEOPLE
- Population: 28,808,658 (1999 est.)
- Major cities: Nairobi, Meru Town, Mombasa
- Language: English (official), Swahili (official)
- Religions: Protestant, Roman Catholic, traditional African religions, Muslim

GOVERNMENT
- Form: Republic
- Head: President
- Legislature: Unicameral National Assembly or Bunge
- Nationhood: December 12, 1963

ECONOMY
- Agricultural Products: Crops—coffee, tea, corn, wheat, sugarcane, fruit, vegetables; dairy products, beef, pork, poultry, eggs. Livestock—camels, cattle, goats, sheep.
- Mining Products: Limestone, fluorspar, salt
- Manufactured Products: Food, beverages, petroleum products, textiles and fibers, garments, tobacco, processed fruits, cement, paper, pyrethrum products, engineering products, wood products, pharmaceuticals, basic chemicals, sugar, rubber, plastics
- Money: Kenyan shilling (1 Kenyan shilling equals 100 cents)

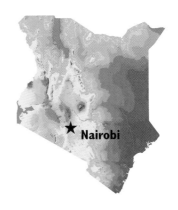

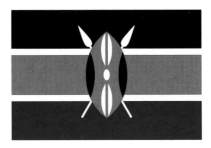

Kenya's flag has three stripes of black, red, and green. The stripes run from top to bottom and are separated by narrow white stripes. The color black represents Kenyans. The color red represents the blood shed in the fight for independence. The color green represents fertility of the land. The color white represents peace. A shield and white spears are in the flag's center. They represent Kenya's pride and tradition.

Timeline

6000 B.C.	Cushites, Bantu, and Nilotes arrive
A.D. 800 - 1400	Arabs and Europeans arrive
LATE 1400s	Portuguese gain control of Kenyan coast
1698	Oman becomes ruling coastal power
1700s	Tribal groups control Kenya
1895	Kenya becomes a British territory
1903	British complete railroad
1920	Kenya becomes a British colony
1920s	Africans form nationalist groups
1929	Jomo Kenyatta goes to England to negotiate Kenya's independence
LATE 1940s	Guerrilla groups form in Kenya
1952	British governor declares state of emergency
1956	Mau Mau rebellion crushed
1960	State of emergency ends
1963	Kenya gains independence
1978	Kenyatta dies; Daniel arap Moi becomes president

Origins

Anthropologist Richard Leakey presents bones he found in Kenya. They are believed to be 1.5 million years old.

Kenya's history stretches back to the origin of human beings. **Archaeological** digs at Koobi Fora uncovered the remains of the ancestor of modern humans. He lived in northern Kenya at least a million years ago!

Ten thousand years ago, small tribal groups called Kenya their home. Each tribe came from different places. These groups were the Kikuyu, Kamba, Luo, and Maasai.

Around 6000 B.C., the Cushites, Bantu, and Nilotes came from the north and west. Superior weapons helped them overwhelm the other tribes. Over many thousands of years, this mix of tribes slowly became the modern peoples of East Africa.

From the ninth to fifteenth centuries, Arabs and Europeans came to Africa. They organized **caravans** into the interior to trade in gold, ivory, and slaves. Arabs built **mosques** and markets in the coastal towns. And, they introduced **Islam**.

In 1593, the Portuguese built Fort Jesus in Mombasa. Today, it is a museum.

By the end of the fifteenth century, the Portuguese had gained control of the Kenyan coast. They ruled until 1698, when Oman became the ruling coastal power.

During the eighteenth century, tribal groups controlled Kenya. Oman continued to rule the coastal cities. But by 1895, Kenya had become a British territory. The British built a railway between Mombasa and Kisumu. This caused fighting between many tribal groups. Many tribal members died.

The railway allowed Europeans to move to Kenya. At first, only hunters and adventurers came. But at the turn of the century, British farmers arrived and set up **plantations**.

The plantations forced many Africans onto inferior land. Others were forced to work on the plantations. **Racial barriers** appeared in business and everyday life. Africans grew to dislike the British.

Jomo Kenyatta

By 1915, the British owned much of the highlands. Africans and Asians could not own land there.

In 1920, Kenya became a British colony. In the 1920s, Africans formed nationalist groups. One of the leaders was Jomo Kenyatta. In 1929, he went to England to discuss Kenya's independence.

During World War II, Africans were forced to fight for the British. Soon after the war, **guerrilla** groups like the Mau Mau were formed. They wanted to expel all white settlers from Kenya. They also wanted to kill Africans who helped the British or benefited from British rule. They raided shops, farms, and police stations.

In 1952, the British governor declared a state of emergency. British troops arrived. They arrested Kenyatta and other leaders of the independence group Kenya African Union (KAU).

The Mau Mau began an armed rebellion. In the next few years, many people died. Prison camps were set up. In 1956, the Mau Mau rebellion was crushed. The leader of the rebellion, Dedan Kimathi, was **executed**.

The rebellion brought changes to Kenya. The restrictions on African farmlands were lifted. A stable middle class began to grow.

In 1960, the state of emergency ended. Britain agreed to meet with African leaders. They discussed the future of the colony.

The KAU reformed into the Kenyan African National Union (KANU). Jomo Kenyatta was released from prison and became its leader.

KANU won the elections in 1963. It voted in favor of a **parliamentary** government. That year, Kenya was granted its independence. Jomo Kenyatta became the country's first president.

Kenyatta's ideas earned him many critics. One was vice-president Oginga Odinga. Odinga was imprisoned, then released after agreeing to join the KANU. In 1969, Tom Mboya, a powerful member of the government, was killed. This led to fighting between the Kikuyu and Luo tribes.

In 1978, Kenyatta died. Daniel arap Moi became president. Moi settled a dispute with Somalia over its borders. He also established relations with Tanzania.

In 1982, the Kenyan Air Force tried to overthrow the government, but was defeated. A new air force was created.

Since that time, Kenya's **economy** has grown slowly but steadily. With the country moving in the right direction, Kenya's future has become much brighter.

The Ancient Land

Rift Valley landscape

Mount Kenya

Kenya is on Africa's eastern coast. It borders Somalia to the east, and Ethiopia and Sudan to the north. To its west is Uganda. Tanzania is on its southern border. The Indian Ocean is on its east coast. Kenya has 225,000 square miles (583,000 sq. km) of land. The **equator** runs through its center.

Kenya has five main areas: the Lake Victoria **basin**, the Central Rift Highlands, the eastern **plateau**, the northern plateau, and the coastal plain.

The Central Rift Valley runs north to south from Lake Turkana to the Tanzanian border. It splits the highlands into two parts. To the Valley's west is the Mau **Escarpment** and the Lake Victoria basin. To the east is the Aberdare Range.

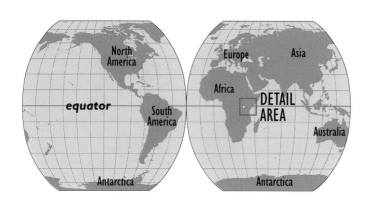

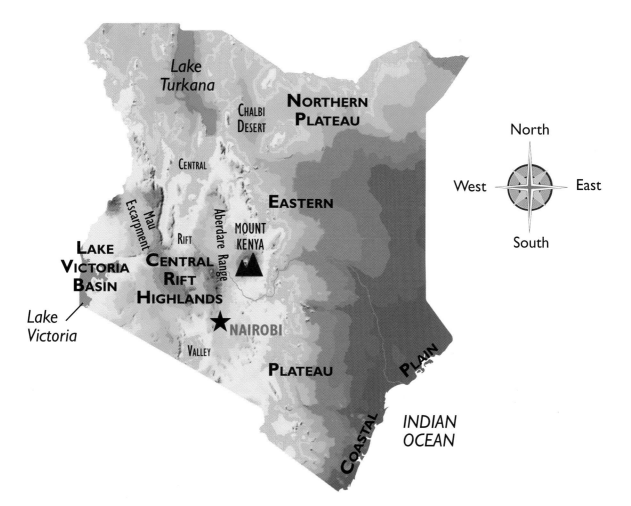

Snow-capped Mount Kenya is also on the eastern side of the Valley. This **extinct** volcano is Kenya's highest point. From there, the eastern **plateau** stretches all the way to the coastal plain.

The northern plateau is Kenya's driest area. Kenya's largest lake, Lake Turkana, is located there. To its east is the Chalbi Desert.

Kenya has a **tropical** climate. Most parts of the country have warm days and cool early mornings and evenings. The coast has high temperatures and **humidity**. It is very dry in the north and northeast parts of the country.

There are two rainy seasons. The long rains last from April to June. The short rains happen from October to December.

Fishing on Lake Victoria

Rainfall

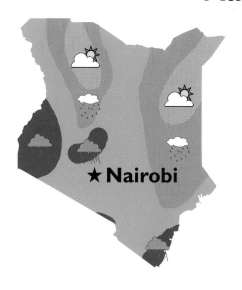

Average Yearly Rainfall

Inches		*Centimeters*
Under 10		**Under 25**
10 - 20		*25 - 50*
20 - 40		*50 - 100*
40 - 60		*100 - 150*
Over 60		*Over 150*

Temperature

Summer

Winter

Average Temperature

Fahrenheit		*Celsius*
Over 68°		**Over 20°**
50° - 68°		*10° - 20°*

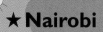

Peculiar Plants

Umbrella acacias grow in Kenya's grasslands. Giraffes enjoy eating the tops of these trees.

Because Kenya has a wide range of climates, it has many kinds of plants. Kenya has more than 40 kinds of acacia trees. Hardwood trees and evergreens are common in the highlands. There are also thick forests and alpine vegetation along the slopes of Mount Kenya.

In higher elevations above the forests, gladioli and heather grow. Here, you can find groundsel trees and the giant lobelia.

In the mountains above 6,000 feet (1,829 m), some areas are covered with dense groves of bamboo, cedar, and juniper. Orchids and flowering creepers grow among the trees.

The giant lobelia can grow to more than 20 feet (6 m) high.

The grasslands to the east and west of the highlands are home to the baobab. Baobabs are also found in the northern desert lands among the thornbush. This tree is part of many African legends.

Baobab trees have huge trunks that can grow to 30 feet (9 m) around.

Along the coast, mangroves grow in the salty water and sandy soil of the swamps. The doum palm tree is also found in Kenya. **Tropical** forests are found in the Arabuko Sokoke Forest Reserve.

The doum palm is special because it has branches. Most palm trees do not.

WILD CREATURES

Kenya has more than 80 kinds of animals and more than 1,000 kinds of birds. More than 160 kinds of **mammals** are found only in Kenya.

The "big five" are the elephant, rhinoceros, buffalo, lion, and leopard. In the early days of the **safari**, these were prized trophies. In 1977, hunting wild animals was banned to save them from **extinction**.

Kenya also has cheetahs, giraffes, hippopotamuses, wildebeests, antelopes, gazelles, impalas, monkeys, hyenas, waterbucks, and many other kinds of animals. And, Kenya is home to the rare green turtle, **endangered** sable, and hirola antelope. Kenya has about 50 national parks and game reserves to protect its wildlife.

ZEBRA

Zebras are horse-like animals, standing 47 to 55 inches (120 to 140 cm) high at the shoulder. They live in plains and open woodland. But in dry seasons, they can be found in woodlands and swamps. The zebra's enemies are lions, hyenas, and humans.

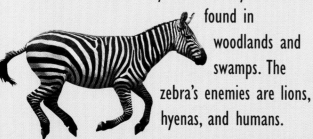

WILDEBEEST

Wildebeests can be 52 inches (1.3 m) tall at the shoulders and weigh 500 pounds (225 kg). They are mostly seen in large herds numbering tens of thousands. Wildebeests are one of the main **herbivores** on the green plains of East Africa.

RHINOCEROS

Kenya has white (left) and black (right) rhinoceroses. After the elephant, rhinos are the world's largest land animals. The white rhinoceros can weigh up to 5.5 tons (4,990 kg). The black can weigh 1.5 tons (1,350 kg). Both live in the grasslands. **Poaching** for their horns has made them nearly **extinct**.

BUFFALO

African buffalos can weigh almost a ton (900 kg). They live in grasslands and mountain forests, usually near water. They move in herds of 500 to 2000, and are dangerous to humans.

HIPPOPOTAMUS

Hippos often weigh up to 4 tons (3,630 kg). They spend much of their lives in the

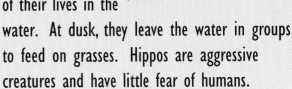

water. At dusk, they leave the water in groups to feed on grasses. Hippos are aggressive creatures and have little fear of humans.

ELEPHANTS

African elephants are the world's largest land animals. They weigh up to 8 tons (7,500 kg). They live mostly in the grasslands in herds of 25 to 30.

CROCODILES

Crocodiles can be more than 20 feet (6 m) long. They live in Kenya's rivers, lakes, and swamps. They spend their days in the water. During the mornings and evenings, they sun themselves on rocks.

LION

Lions weigh 287 to 485 pounds (130 to 220 kg). They are the most powerful **predators** in East Africa. They live in **prides** of related females.

LEOPARD

Leopards weigh 110 to 200 pounds (50 to 90 kg). They live in rocky mountain areas and forests. During the day, Leopards rest in tree branches. They hunt at night.

CHEETAH

The cheetah's thin body and long legs are designed for speed. Cheetahs weigh only 100 to 140 pounds (45 to 64 kg). But, they are the fastest animals in the world. They can run more than 70 mph (112 km/h).

BABOONS

Baboons weigh 30 to 88 pounds (14 to 40 kg). Baboons spend much of their time on the ground. They only go into the trees at night to sleep. Baboons live in grasslands, forests, and **plateaus**.

GIRAFFE

Giraffes are found in the grasslands. They are the world's tallest animal. Giraffes can be 18 feet (5.5 m) tall and weigh more than a ton (900 kg).

HYENA

Hyenas can be 3 feet (1 m) tall. They hunt in large packs. Their strong jaws can bite through almost anything, even bone. Hyenas will eat any animal they can bring down.

BIRDS

The ostrich lives on the plains in pairs or flocks of up to 50. It is the world's largest and heaviest bird. It stands up to 8 feet (2.5 m) tall and weighs 300 pounds (136 kg). The ostrich cannot fly. But, it can run up to 40 mph (64 km/h).

The secretary bird stands 4 feet (1.2 m) tall. It searches through the tall grasses for small **mammals** and **reptiles** to eat.

Vultures are often seen in grassland trees. They can be 39 inches (100 cm) long and weigh 28 pounds (12 kg). They eat dead animals.

Hornbills can be 60 inches (160 cm) long. They have long beaks and tails, and broad wings. They nest in the holes of hollowed trees, and wall up the tree hole with mud.

The lakes of the Rift Valley are home to the greatest grouping of birds. Thousands of pink flamingos cover the shallow beds of Lake Nakuru.

Lake Baringo is home to herons, storks, cranes (right), and a variety of kingfishers.

A Tribal People

A Bantu man and his son

Over the centuries, people from many parts of Africa have moved to Kenya. Arabs, Asians, and Europeans also live there. Kenya has more than 50 **ethnic** groups and 80 different **dialects**. Kenya's African population can be divided into three main groups: Bantu, Nilotic, and Cushitic.

The Bantu tribes are the largest in Kenya. Bantu groups include the Kikuyu, Embu, Meru, Mbeeri, Kemba, and Tharaka. Most Bantu people live in the south. Some farm in the Central Rift Highlands.

The largest group of Nilotic peoples are called the Luo. They settled around the shores of Lake Victoria. They farm and fish for a living. Luo politicians played a major part in Kenya's struggle for independence.

Other Nilotic tribes include the Maasai, Samburu, Turkana, and Kalenjin. The Maasai roam southern Kenya with their herds. The

Samburu live in central Kenya. The Turkana live in the northwest. The Kalenjin are settled farmers who live in the Rift Valley region.

Samburu kids

Only a small part of Kenya's population is Cushitic. They include the Somalis and the Oromo. Cushitic **nomads** roam the northern region of the country.

Kenya has no official religion. But most Kenyans belong to the Roman Catholic, Anglican, or Protestant church. Kenya also has a large **Muslim** population. Some Kenyans still follow tribal religions.

Many different tribal languages are spoken in Kenya. Kenya's two official languages are English and Swahili. Swahili is a language made up of several other languages such as Bantu, Arabic, Portuguese, and English.

A Maasai girl in traditional clothing

All Kenyan students must pay to go to school. Kenyan children are not required to attend school. But over the years, more and more children have enrolled. Children go to eight years of primary school. Then, they

A Kenyan school

attend four years of secondary school. If they wish, they may go on to college.

Some schools in Kenya are called *Harambee* schools. They are run by the community. Today, there are more *Harambee* schools than government-funded schools.

Most Kenyans live in small, thatched-roof houses with dirt floors. The walls are often made of mud or bundles of branches. In the cities, Kenyans live in houses or apartment buildings made of stone or cement.

A Kenyan house with a well

Chapati

2 cups flour
1 teaspoon salt
Oil (or butter)

Sift flour and salt into a bowl. Add enough water to make a stiff dough. Knead well. Roll out on a floured board into a thick circle. Brush with oil. From the center of the circle, make a cut to one edge. Roll up dough into a cone, press both ends in, and make a ball again. Repeat that process 2-3 more times. Divide dough into 4 or 5 balls, and roll each out into a thin circle. Heat a frying pan over moderate heat and dry out each chapati in the pan quickly. Brush pan with oil and fry chapati slowly until golden brown on each side. Serve hot or cold with stew or sauce. Makes 4 servings.

AN IMPORTANT NOTE TO THE CHEF: Always have an adult help with the preparation and cooking of food. Never use kitchen utensils or appliances without adult permission and supervision.

The Growing Business

A Maasai herdsman

Farming is Kenya's main **industry**. The main crops are coffee, tea, pyrethrum, and maize. Farmers also grow sugarcane, wheat, sorghum, beans, and bananas. There are dairy farms and livestock ranches, too.

Most farming is done in the highlands where there is enough rainfall to raise crops. Wheat farms are found on the Rift Valley **plateaus**. Farms on the northern, northeastern, and southern plains also raise livestock.

The fishing industry is confined to the coast and Lake Victoria. Forestry is a major industry in the rainy parts of the highlands.

The tourism industry is an important part of Kenya's **economy**. Most visitors come to Kenya for a grassland **safari** to see the many animals. Tourists can take a safari at more than 45 national parks and game reserves.

Visitors on a safari can see Kenya's wildlife up close.

Kenya has a well-established communication system. Kenya Posts and **Telecommunications** Corporation provides international telephone service, mobile telephones, telex, facsimile, and data communication.

A woman harvests tea

Kenya's major **industries** are in Mombasa and Nairobi. Most manufacturers process farm products. There are also meat processors and dairy industries. Other industries include leather, paper, textile, and sugar production.

Oil products are made at government-owned **refineries** on the coast. Kenya relies on **imported** oil for its jet and diesel fuel. Imported raw materials are used to make machinery and motor vehicles.

Kenya has limited mineral **resources**. Alkaline deposits from hot springs are mined for soda ash. The soda ash is then used in glass-making. Building stone is made from volcanic rock. Limestone deposits along the coast are used to make cement. Coal production supports small steel mills.

Urban Places

Nairobi

Nairobi was founded in the late 1890s. It was a British railroad camp on the Mombasa-to-Uganda railroad. From 1899 to 1905, it served as a British **provincial** capital. In 1905, the city became the capital of the British East Africa Protectorate. In 1920, its name changed to Kenya Colony. In 1963, Nairobi became the capital of independent Kenya.

Nairobi is in the southern highlands. It is Kenya's main **economic**, administrative, and **cultural** center. And it is one of the largest and fastest growing cities in Africa.

Manufactured products include processed food, textiles, clothing, building materials, and communications and transportation equipment. The city also has a large tourism

industry. The University of Nairobi, Kenya Polytechnic, and Kenya Conservatory of Music are there.

Meru Town is located on the northeast slopes of Mount Kenya, about five miles (8 km) north of the **equator**. It is located in a forested area with smaller towns, villages, and farms.

Meru Town is a business, agricultural, and educational center for northeastern Kenya. It has several banks and many hotels, markets, and transportation terminals. Coffee, tea, timber, cattle, and other goods are produced in Meru Town. There are teacher training colleges and the Kenya Methodist University.

Mombasa is the chief seaport of Kenya. It is on a bay in the Indian Ocean, just south of the equator. Old Mombasa is located on a small offshore island. There is also a larger, more modern mainland metropolitan area. It is connected to the island by a bridge and ferry boats.

A view of Mombasa from the old section to the new section

Getting Around

Many kinds of vehicles travel on Nairobi's roads.

Telecommunications and airlines link Kenya with the rest of the world. A network of roads and railway lines connects Kenya with Tanzania, Uganda, Sudan, Ethiopia, and Somalia.

Buses and mini-buses connect Kenya's cities. There are bus services between Nairobi and all other towns.

Kenya has a large road network that connects most of the country. Paved roads connect all major cities. They handle about half of Kenya's freight traffic.

Kenya has a single-track railway system running from Mombasa through Nairobi to Uganda, with branches to Nanyuki, Kitale, and

Nairobi train station

Kisumu. Another branch connects Kenya to Tanzania through Taveta. There's a branch running from Nakuru to Kisumu on Lake Victoria. And, another runs from Nairobi to Nanyuki near Mount Kenya.

Kenya has a well-developed air transportation system. It has international airports in Nairobi and Mombasa and more than 150 airstrips throughout the country.

Country roads

Nairobi's Jomo Kenyatta International Airport serves more than 30 airlines, including Kenya's national airline, Kenya Airways. The airport provides direct scheduled flights to major capitals in Europe, the Middle East, and Asia. Wilson Airport in Nairobi handles light aircraft, and is one of the busiest airports in Africa.

A Kenya Airways airplane rests at the Jomo Kenyatta airport.

Government

The president and **cabinet** govern Kenya with the support of **parliament**. The parliament is the only lawmaking body in Kenya.

The parliament has a single chamber known as the National Assembly. It has 210 elected members and 12 members chosen by the president to represent social and **economic** interests.

Kenya's constitution grants citizenship, and protects the rights and freedom of individuals. Kenya's constitution was introduced on December 12, 1963.

There are eight **provinces** in Kenya. Each is divided into districts. The provinces are the Central, Coast, Eastern, Nairobi, North East, Nyanza, Rift Valley, and Western. The smallest is the Nairobi Province. The largest are the Eastern and Rift Valley Provinces. The Nairobi Province has the most people. The North East has the fewest.

Kenya's currency is the shilling. It is divided into 100 cents. There are paper notes in the following units: 10, 20, 50, 100, 500, and 1000 shillings.

A Kenyan 10-shilling note. President Daniel arap Moi is on the front (top). The University of Nairobi and Mount Kenya are on the back.

Holidays & Festivals

Jamhuri, on December 12, is Kenya's biggest national holiday. It celebrates Kenya's independence from Great Britain in 1963.

Jamhuri is celebrated nationwide. But there are special events in Nairobi. You can hear speeches by the president and other officials. There are parades, fireworks, and *ngomas*, which are dances performed in public plazas.

On October 5 is the Nairobi Show. Everyone looks forward to this yearly agricultural and technological fair. It is Africa's largest.

It is an honor for farmers to be chosen to display prize potatoes, cabbages, carrots, or cattle there. They also show other farmers how to grow more crops. There are also weaving and pottery demonstrations.

President Daniel arap Moi of Kenya inspects a guard of honor during the 36th anniversary of independence, known as Jamhuri Day, December 12, 1999, in Nairobi.

Sports & Leisure

A Kenyan runner trains for his next race.

Kenyans compete in many different sports. Kenya's world-respected track and long distance runners have won countless medals at the Olympic Games and at track meets worldwide. Kenya's **cricketers** have competed successfully in World Cup events, including an upset of the West Indies team in 1996.

The Harambee Stars, Kenya's national soccer team, qualified for the second round of the 1998 World Cup. Club teams have competed in regional tournaments.

Rugby is also a popular sport. Kenya has some of the best golf courses on the continent, too. Kenya's annual Safari Rally is one of the most exciting rally events in Africa.

There are a wide range of other sports and hobbies. There is sport-fishing, mountain climbing, riding, sailing, and some of the world's best bird watching.

Music lovers will find everything from gospel, rumba, and rock to **acoustic** guitar. Kenya still values **traditional** rhythms like *chakacha,* which is a type of dance. And, there are ancient instruments like the *nyatiti,* a string instrument.

Nairobi National Park is a large wildlife preserve on the edge of Nairobi. It is a major tourist attraction. Nairobi also has the National Museum of Kenya. It is known for its display on early humans in Africa. Tourists also like to see the **parliament** buildings, the law courts, City Hall, the city park, McMillan Memorial Library, the busy Municipal Market and nearby bazaar, the Kenya National Theatre, and Sorsbie Art Gallery.

Kenya's coastline is famous for its hundreds of miles of clean, sandy, palm-lined beaches. The coast has many hotels and resorts. With so many national treasures, it's no wonder Kenya has become a favorite destination for tourists around the world.

Trees surround a lake in Nairobi city park.

Glossary

acoustic - something used to absorb and deaden sound.

archaeology - the study of people, customs, and life in ancient times.

basin - all the land drained by a river and the streams that flow into it.

cabinet - a group of advisors chosen by the head of a nation to direct certain departments of government.

caravan - a group such as merchants, pilgrims, or tourists often traveling together for safety through difficult or dangerous country.

cricket - an English outdoor game played by two teams of eleven players, with a ball, bats, and wickets.

culture - the customs, arts, and tools of a nation or people at a certain time.

dialect - a form of a language spoken in a certain district or by a certain group of people.

economy - the way a country manages its resources.

endangered - an animal that could soon become extinct.

equator - an imaginary circle around the middle of the earth.

escarpment - a steep slope or cliff.

ethnic - of or having to do with a group of people who have the same race, nationality, or culture.

execute - to put to death according to law.

extinct - no longer existing.

guerrilla - a member of a band of fighters, usually not part of a regular army, who combat the enemy with sudden attacks.

habitat - a place where a living thing is naturally found.

herbivore - any animal that feeds on plants.

humidity - moistness or dampness of the atmosphere.

import - to bring in goods from a foreign country for sale or use.

industry - any form of business, manufacture, or trade.

Islam - the religion based on the teachings of the prophet Mohammed.

mammal - a warm-blooded animal with a backbone and hair.

mosque - a Muslim place of worship.

Muslim - a follower of the prophet Mohammed and Islam.

nomad - a member of a tribe that moves around from place to place in search of food or pasture for its cattle.

parliament - the highest lawmaking body of the Kenyan government.

plantation - a large farm or estate on which cotton, tobacco, sugarcane, or rubber tress are grown.

plateau - a plain in the mountains.

poach - to hunt or fish illegally.

predator - an animal that kills and eats other animals.
pride - a group of lions.
province - one of the main divisions of a country.
racial barrier - restrictions of a person's human or civil rights because of his or her race.
refinery - the building and machinery for purifying sugar, petroleum, and other things.
reptile - a cold-blooded animal with scales, a backbone, and lungs.
resource - the actual and possible wealth of a country.
rugby - a form of football played with an oval ball by two fifteen-person teams.
safari - a journey or hunting expedition.
telecommunication - the science or study of sending messages over long distances by electronic means.
tradition - the handing down of beliefs, customs, and stories from parents to children.
tropics - regions near the equator; the warmest regions on earth.

Swahili   English

Jambo _____	Hello
Kwaheri_____	Good-bye
Tafadhali _____	Please
Asante _____	Thank you
Naam_____	Yes
Siyo _____	No
Ndovu _____	Elephant
Simba_____	Lion

LANGUAGE

Web Sites

For general information about Kenya, visit KenyaWeb at:
http://www.kenyaweb.com

Yale University has a Swahili to English online dictionary:
http://www.yale.edu/swahili/abc/se_N.html

These sites are subject to change. Go to your favorite search engine and type in "Kenya" for more sites.

Index